Santiago de Compostela

- The Way of Saint James -

by
David Baldwin

*All booklets are published thanks to the
generous support of the members of the
Catholic Truth Society*

CATHOLIC TRUTH SOCIETY
PUBLISHERS TO THE HOLY SEE

Contents

∽

*I felt the fatigue, hunger and pain of those hundreds
of thousands who have gone before.
I felt their presence. I also shared their joy, awe and elation.*

*I share it all with my fellow pilgrims
as we travelled the Way together.*

*That small part of me left behind
will share with those who come after.*

*This little book is dedicated to those pilgrims who have
followed, are following, or will follow the Way of Saint
James to Santiago de Compostela.*

With grateful thanks to the Very Revd Daniel Rees OSB of Downside
Abbey, and Laurie Dennett, Chairman of the Confraternity of St James.

PREFACE

I am honoured to introduce this excellent book on the Way of Saint James *(El Camino de Santiago)*, the resting place of the Apostle. Every pilgrimage implies a voyage of self-discovery and a search for something greater and beyond oneself. The pilgrimage to the tomb of Saint James was for many centuries a meeting point for those devoted to the Saint who, through the penance of pilgrimage, affirmed Christendom, the *Respublica Christiana*, then threatened by internal and external enemies.

Today's pilgrims, so much part of a modern and fundamentally urbanised world, must abandon it to meet nature along paths which both physically and spiritually diverge from everyday life. So they experience the same uprooting as their predecessors of centuries past. Even more so! For such a pilgrim journey is precisely the opposite of the daily, routine trips of modern suburbia – often underground, stifling, crowded but very much alone, as compared to the easy companionship over mountains and valleys, under sunshine and rain, moving towards a meaningful end.

A debt of gratitude is certainly owed to the author, David Baldwin, for providing such a scholarly and fascinating book which will help both seasoned pilgrim and attract those who have still to make the journey.

The Marqués de Tamarón, Ambassador of Spain to the Court of St James, Easter 2001

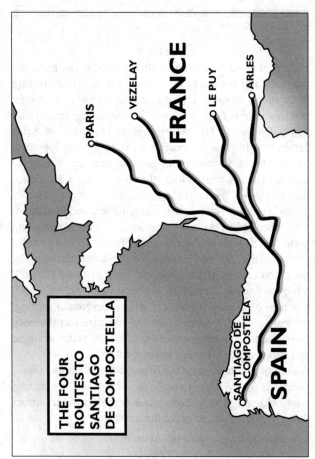

THE FOUR
ROUTES TO
SANTIAGO
DE COMPOSTELLA

PILGRIM WAYS

"Pilgrimages symbolise the experience of the *homo viator* who sets out, as soon as he leaves the maternal womb, on his journey through the time and space of his existence. This is the fundamental experience of Israel, which is marching towards the promised land of salvation and of full freedom; the experience of Christ who rose to heaven from the land of Jerusalem, thus opening the way towards the Father; the experience of the Church which moves on through history towards the heavenly Jerusalem; the experience of the whole of humankind which tends towards hope and fullness". This powerful, all-embracing view of pilgrimage is the summary of *'The Great Pilgrimage in the Jubilee'* issued by the Pontifical Council for the Pastoral Care of Migrants and Itinerant Peoples, and approved by Pope John Paul II in April 1998.

It is a far cry from the immediate and popular images that come to mind with the word 'pilgrimage' - either that of the Chaucerian band of rowdy, somewhat irreligious folk on their way to Canterbury, or, the other Middle Age image of the solitary pilgrim with his long robe, wide hat, staff, gourd and pouch, tramping under a leaden sun or fighting through a whipping snow storm, in a resigned, weary, but noble way, to some far-off holy destination.

Early beginnings - Rome and Jerusalem

Whatever the definition or image, the urge to make the physical pilgrim-journey goes back beyond the memory of man. It has been proposed that among primitive tribes people who, for whatever reason, had wandered from the influence of their local deity, were driven to return to their geographical roots for divine assistance or inspiration; so, the mountain man returned to the mountains, the river person his river area. An anonymous and contemporary poem painted on a factory wall along the Way of St James on the approach to Najera, in Spain, sums up this primitive urge:

"The force that drives me/ the force that draws me
I am unable to explain/ Only He Above knows!".

In pre-Christian days the practice of journeying to holy places is well documented. The Egyptians journeyed to Sekket's shrine at Bubastis; the Greeks sought inspiration from Apollo at Delphi, the Peruvians massed to worship the sun at Cuzco.

It is ironic that the first Christian pilgrimage was made, and still is, to an empty tomb - that from which Jesus rose; and it is this empty tomb that still commands the most interest and inspiration. Those first pilgrims were probably local folk: a mixture of the plain curious and those who came to marvel - and believe.

There is no firm evidence of any great pilgrim movement to Jerusalem from further afield during the first three centuries after the death of Jesus, for indeed the city was destroyed by Titus in 70AD, and it took many decades to be rebuilt. Believers, certainly in the first century AD, were also probably more preoccupied with the Parousia, the anticipated Second Coming of Christ. The new Church was also devoting its energies to looking outwards and establishing itself, as instructed by Christ, to "Go, therefore make disciples of all nations" *(Mt 28:19)*.

However, Jerusalem was firmly put on the map when Constantine the Great, the first Christian Roman emperor, built the Church of the Holy Sepulchre on the supposed site of the tomb, early in the fourth century, and pilgrimage to Jerusalem was given prominence by the visit of the Empress Helena, Constantine's mother. Since those early days, Jerusalem has been, and will no doubt remain, the most significant and spiritual Christian pilgrim site for the most compelling reason: as put by Origen, "to walk in the footsteps of the Master".

The destruction of Jerusalem, and the spread of the Church by Dispersion through the Roman Empire, also effectively destroyed this embryonic focal point for the young Christian Church. From then on, all paths, physically and spiritually, effectively led to Rome. The martyrdom of Ss Peter and Paul, and many others, during the Neronian persecutions of 64-67AD laid a strong basis for this. So, after the early pilgrimages to the Holy Land, Rome, as a growing Christian centre, was soon established as a prominent pilgrim venue. "If I were freed from my labours and my body were in sound health I would eagerly make a pilgrimage merely to see the chains that held him captive and the prison where he lay", says St John Chrysostom longingly in the context of his great love for St Paul at the end of the fourth century.

Growth of Pilgrimages

Apart from the increasing passage to the Holy Land, and latterly Rome, other forms of pilgrimage in the first millennium appear unstructured and fragmented. In the early Church it was often motivated by a desire for exile and renunciation of civilisation. Hence, in this context, the hermit was regarded as a pilgrim soul by St Jerome, and the establishment of the very early monasteries was perceived as an extension of this principle of the pilgrimage of exile. The mobile pilgrims of the times were those who left their homes, as did the exilic Irish monks of the sixth and seventh centuries, to wander at will and without particular destination, on the principle of "exile for God's sake, and go not only to Jerusalem, but everywhere, for God is everywhere".

Late in the first millennium and on into the second, all this began to change. The Church had consolidated into an organised power centred on Rome. The Christianised

Empire had expanded into central and northern Europe and up to the Baltic states, as well as to the East. Churches were being built or rebuilt, and overland routes were being further developed and extended. The establishment of local theophanies through the veneration of Jesus, Mary and the saints at these churches, along with a growing relic cult - particularly those of martyrs, started drawing pilgrims to their sites - to places "where God made His power especially manifest". Pilgrimage began to be ritualised and formalised by such acts as the granting of indulgences and selling of pardons; sinners and criminals were sentenced by church or court to undergo penitential pilgrimages. One of the better known penitential pilgrimages was that of Henry II to Rome in atonement for the murder of Thomas a Becket. These developments of pilgrimage were all part-manifestation of a Church strengthening its identity and universality, and in more earthly terms, its political and economic power.

Great Age of Pilgrimage

Through this growing popularity and prominence, the Middle Ages became the Great Age of pilgrimage. Rome and Jerusalem vied with each other as premier destinations, and with vigorous and shrewd promotion by its Archbishops, particularly Archbishop Gelmirez *(1100-1140)*, Santiago de Compostela came to rank with these two as one of the great destinations of medieval pilgrimage. In the twelfth and thirteenth centuries half a million people in some years have been said to have made the pilgrimage from all over Europe to venerate St James.

Wherever the destination, the pilgrim journey was typically a lengthy and hazardous affair. The pilgrim routes were badly constructed and poorly marked, crossing harsh, unforgiving and often mountainous terrain, with accompanying extremes of weather and wild beasts in the remote parts. Safe passage was by no means assured, and in the frequent isolated areas, robbers and bandits preyed.

The bandit problem became serious enough for the issue of a Pontifical document *'In Coena Domini'* in 1303, anathematising bandits who attacked pilgrims. In populated areas pilgrims were often prey to more insidious threats - those from unscrupulous innkeepers and pseudo pilgrims - the coquillards - who befriended and then robbed their erstwhile companions.

Dangers and Preparations

Wars prevailed in many parts - the pilgrimage to Rome went into serious decline in the 10th and 13th centuries through large scale unrest en route, as did the pilgrimage to Santiago on account of the 100 Years War. Jerusalem, and the Holy Sepulchre, seized by the Turks in 1078 put paid to pilgrimage there, and was one reason why Santiago became a popular alternative venue. Disease was rife, treatment non-existent or at best, primitive. Food and fodder were scarce, and along certain points of the Way to Santiago, poisonous water was a hazard. But to many, this was all grist to the mill: the more hazardous the route, the greater the merit and grace, which pilgrims believed would be their due. Pilgrims were also expected to journey in a state of poverty, "My possessions are a sack on my shoulders with a bit of dry bread and a Holy Bible that I carry under my shirt. No other thing do I have." *(The Way of The Pilgrim, Anonymous Russian)*. The well-off made large and generous donations to compensate for their fortunate circumstances. As a result of all the hazards, pilgrims tended to start travelling together in large, and sometimes, raucous bands, reminiscent of Chaucer's pilgrims. Bishops or noblemen on pilgrimage were popular, and attracted many hangers-on and individual pilgrims who wished to travel in their protective company.

With some foreknowledge of all this, the prudent pilgrim made thorough arrangements before setting off. He was required to make amends by apology or in kind to all those he had offended or deprived. A sincere confession should then follow, otherwise the pilgrimage, for all its physical and moral accomplishments, would be spiritually worthless. A pilgrim's will had a special and protected status. A specific length of time would be decreed, on the expiry of which he would be deemed deceased, and his wife free to remarry. In one part of Normandy this period was a year and a day, after which his will was automatically executed. The pilgrim, with his staff and scrip (leather pouch), would certainly expect a holy blessing before final departure.

Hospitality en route

Amongst all these vicissitudes, the one glimmer of relief for the pilgrim was the hope of hospitality along the route, "for all pilgrims, rich or poor, who go to St James ought to be received with charity by all. Whoever receives them, receives St James and God himself", is the reassuring statement in the Pilgrim's Guide to Santiago, the *Codex Calixtinus*. The main burden in dispensing this hospitality naturally fell on the religious orders of the time. It was incorporated in the Benedictine Rule. Other Orders, if not dispensing charity, had specific tasks in support of the pilgrimage, such as the Frères Pontiff, who were responsible for building and maintaining the bridges along the pilgrim route, the bridge over the River Lot at Espalion being a fine example.

With the burgeoning demand from the hundreds of thousands of pilgrims along the major routes there was invariably, by the middle of the 12th century, a pilgrim hospice or hospital within a day's travel of each other. Life in these austere establishments was reported as "monstrous and uncomfortable". Some provided basic victuals; beds were a rarity, straw on the floor was the norm. The well-off paid their way, some worked for their keep, but this prolonged the journey. The prize for hypocrisy must go to those wealthy folk who stayed safely at home whilst their paid, proxy pilgrim endured the hazards and earned the indulgence for their benefactor.

Pilgrim's Clothing

The gradual formalising process of pilgrimage during the twelfth and thirteenth centuries also saw the evolution of the pilgrim's garb into something of a distinctive uniform that served the purpose of setting him apart from the ordinary traveller. The details of these are famously described by Sir Walter Raleigh:

"Give me my scallop shell of quiet.
My staff of faith to walk upon,
My scrip of joy, immortal diet,
My bottle of salvation
My gown of glory (hope's true gage),
And then I'll take my pilgrimage,"

added to which is the now familiar broad brimmed hat turned up at the front, frequently featured on images of St James.

By the 14th and 15th centuries the pilgrim's 'uniform' had evolved a distinctive and ornate symbolism. Many venues attracted their own token or badge, which the returning pilgrim wore, diplaying where he had been, and signifiying that he was entitled to continuing hospitality as a *bona fide* pilgrim.

One of the other reasons for going on pilgrimage in those times was to escape from the confinements of daily life, which, on the spiritual front, may have been dominated by the strictures of the parish priest, through whom lay the only route to salvation. One wonders, given the hazards of pilgrimage, whether this escape was after all warranted. There is also evidence, that although pilgrims journeyed well beyond the confines of their highly localised lifestyle, pilgrimage itself was no great broadener of the mind. Pilgrims generally mistrusted and were unable to understand the local people; they in turn were either regarded as a nuisance in the same light as today's modern tourist hordes, or as a means of making a lucrative living.

Controversy

By the late Middle Ages Rome was the most popular destination, chiefly through the presence of the Pope as St Peter's successor. There was, however, a pervading feeling that 'tourism' was beginning to creep in as the motivating factor, thinly disguised as pilgrimage - material curiosity was beginning to replace the deep spiritual motives of those pre 15th century pilgrims. This was described as 'curiositas', curiosity of the worldly, preventing concentration on the divine. 'Official arrangements' were now being made for pilgrims' travel; pilgrims themselves were becoming more knowledgeable, demanding, and less humble. 15th century pilgrims were "creatures of passing fads" visiting obscure shrines which subsequently relapsed into obscurity. Local saints came into vogue, as did veneration of recently deceased, popular parish priests.

Throughout this whole period of early Christian pilgrimage there also runs a thread of unease for the necessity of physical pilgrimage. Even St John Chrysostom, generally an ardent supporter of pilgrimage, commented on one occasion that there was, "need for none to cross the seas or fare upon a long journey; let each of us at home invoke God earnestly and He will hear our prayer". St Augustine observed that, "not by journeying but by loving we draw nigh unto God. To Him who is everywhere present and everywhere entire we approach not by our feet but by our hearts". Later on in the period, the 13th century Franciscan preacher Berthold of Ratisbon, was fearful that some pilgrims might return as even worse sinners, summed up by the mediaeval proverb, "Go a pilgrim, return a whore".

This last remark echoed the fact that however noble the pilgrimage concept was, and indeed nobly executed by many, the practicalities often fell far short of any Christian ideal. For corruption and fraudulence were at times endemic at all levels and all along the pilgrim routes. From the Church came an unprecedented degree of 'discoveries' of relics onwards from the 11th century all over Europe, as local bishops observed the growing popularity of the pilgrimage movement and attempted to jump on the band wagon. From the pilgrim routes came the unscrupulous innkeepers and fraudulent pardoners preying on the gullibility and vulnerability of the pilgrim, but compounding this was widespread prostitution, an over abundance of alcohol and other vices. It was not as though this was going unnoticed, though, as Gregory the Great recognised: "Rascality, adultery, theft, idolatry, poisoning, quarrelling and murder are rife".

Decline of great pilgrimages

The second half of the second millennium saw the decline of the great pilgrimages. There were many reasons for this. The Reformation played a principal part, particularly at the hands of those Reformers such as the arch-satirist Erasmus, who in his *'Religious Pilgrimage'* poured out contempt and derision, playing greatly on the abuses evident in the pilgrimage world. He pointed out the irresponsibility of the happily wandering pilgrims neglecting their duties at home, the advantages taken of the hapless pilgrims by the unscrupulous, the over zealousness of the keepers of the shrines, and the fraud. At the hands of such a master wordsmith a damning indictment of the pilgrim practice was constructed.

Luther was more direct, blunt and persistent in his views: "Pilgrimages should be stopped", and listed many pilgrimage churches that, "should be levelled". In quoting Acts 4:12 "Only in him is there salvation; for of all the names in the world given to men, this is the only one by which we can be saved", going on to assert, "thus there is no analogy between Christ and James of Compostela, therefore I reject James as an idol". He railed against what he saw as the current view of Christ as awesome judge rather than loving saviour, and branded the veneration of the saints as putting them up as rivals to Christ. He advocated "justification by faith, not by pilgrimage".

In keeping with the Reformers' overall views of man and his direct relationship with God through the Bible, perfect pilgrimage should therefore be an interior journey, a shift from external to internal, words replacing walking, meditation in place of marching. As for the granting of pardons and indulgences, "What should I say of them that hug themselves with their counterfeit pardons" was Luther's rebuke.

In 1538 Henry VIII required all who had praised pilgrimage to publicly retract. Those who continued their allegiance to Rome, whilst recognising the abuses of pilgrimage, along with the need for reform of the Church in general, nonetheless mounted a stout defence of pilgrimage in Europe and Britain. Thomas More was prominent with such reminders that pilgrimage centres were authentic places where God may be encountered, and that an honest pilgrimage was at the very least a reminder and re-enactment of the life of Christ and the Saints.

The immediate effect of Reformation was an overall downturn in pilgrimages. There were little, if any Protestant pilgrims, whilst Catholic pilgrimage continued, but in a subdued and diminished manner. In addition to the verbal attacks and outright ban imposed by the

Reformers, there were continuing practical obstacles such as the Wars of Religion between Catholics and Huguenots, 1562-98, which prevented geographical passage. Movement to Santiago was depressed when St James's relics had to be hidden during the period when Drake's raids (1585-1587) threatened coastal areas; pilgrim movement was also severely restricted during the Napoleonic conquest of the Iberian Peninsula (1808-1814). Scepticism and anti-clericalism started to prevail, reinforced by such events as the great earthquake of Lisbon in 1755 on All Saints Day, which evinced a degree of cynicism over saintly patronage and protection which was so mightily lauded at the time! All this could have been summed up by the self-righteous saying: "All ye that seek St James and saints of Rome seeketh St Truth, for he may save you alone".

Renaissance in pilgrimge

Thus, the fortunes of pilgrimage fluctuated during the seventeenth and eighteenth centuries. The counter Reformation added some stimulus in the eighteenth century, but the great era of massed pilgrimage had controversially and finally drawn to a close. The success of pilgrimage had been perverted by human greed, and it fell victim to that success. But this muted close did not reckon with that innate and mysterious human desire to make physical journey to visit holy places. The nineteenth and twentieth centuries saw a gradual renaissance in pilgrimage, re-emerging from many different directions and in many different guises. Tourist travel was becoming safer and more widely available, and commercial tour operators saw a market for organised pilgrimages. Thomas Cook is a notable example, with his organising the first pilgrimage to the Holy Land in 1869 soon after the opening of the Suez canal. There was now a blurring of the pilgrim and the tourist, mirroring that strange irony of those first visitors to that empty tomb - a combination of the curious and the devout.

There was also a resurgence of Protestant pilgrimage, partly inspired by the British military campaign in Palestine in 1916/17. Scholastic and archaeological interest also renewed interest in visiting the holy places, and the ever recurring theme was now taken up by Evelyn Waugh, "The pilgrim's instinct is deep set in the human heart rather than of the head". Another phenomenon also occurred which brought new meaning and new impetus to pilgrimage - the Apparitions of Our Lady at various places throughout the world: 1858 at Lourdes and 1917 in Fatima are two major examples, and with as yet unapproved but ongoing events at Medjugorje, which has drawn an estimated twenty million visitors since the reported Apparitions started in 1981.

All these places are hugely popular, usually drawing their pilgrims in by plane, train, coach and car. The Holy Land and Rome, for the obvious reasons, predominate,

although the troubles in Palestine and Israel leave a continuing question mark and blight over the holy sites of the
three big world faiths. Local pilgrimages, such as those to
Walsingham and Canterbury Cathedral flourish, as do their
counterparts elsewhere in the world. Santiago de
Compostela, regarded as the third great pilgrim venue, continues to increase in popularity, and its particular appeal is
that it is the one remaining pilgrimage with an established
and frequent infrastructure along its main routes that not
only cater for the modern pilgrim, but also reproduce the
long distance walking pilgrimages of the great age.

Pilgrimage has found its place again. From those early
Christians who were making their allegorical journey to re-
enact the life of Christ, to the pilgrim of the Middle Ages
caught up with the desire to seek pardon and indulgence, to
the modern pilgrim/tourist who go for a great variety of
reasons ranging from the curiositas to the deeply devoted.

> Thus far did I come laden with my sin,
> Nor could aught ease the grief that I was in
> Till I came hither.
> What a place is this!
> Must here be the beginning of my bliss?
> Must here the burden fall off from my back?
> Must here the strings that bound it to me crack?
> Blest Cross! Blest Sepulchre! Blest, rather, be
> The Man that there was put to shame for me!
> (John Bunyan, The Pilgrim's Progress)

SAINT JAMES THE GREATER
AND SANTIAGO DE COMPOSTELA

James the brother of John

"Going on from there he saw another pair of brothers, James son of Zebedee and his brother John; they were in their boat with their father Zebedee, mending their nets, and he called them. And at once, leaving the boat and their father, they followed him" *(Mt 4:21,22)*. Thus James enters the New Testament at an early stage as one of the twelve Apostles *(see also Mk 1:19,20 and Lk 5:10,11)*. In the lists of the Apostles in the Gospels the names of Peter and Andrew, James and John are the first four to be mentioned. They have been described as a prominent and chosen group, particularly Peter, James and John.

It was these three who were present at key events in Jesus' ministry: the raising of Jairus's daughter *(Mk 5:37; Lk 8:51)*, the Transfiguration *(Mk 9:1; Mt 17:1; Lk 9:28)*, and in the Garden of Gethsemane *(Mt 26:37; Mk 14:33)* during Our Lord's Agony. The fact that James's name mostly appears before that of his brother, John, has been taken as implication that he is the elder of the two. They both had the singular distinction of being given a personal and endearing nickname, *Boanerges* - Sons of Thunder - by Our Lord *(Mk 3:17)*, indicating their great pent up energies and strength of character.

After the first Pentecost and dispersion of the Apostles to preach and evangelise, there is no firm documentary evidence that James carried his mission to the Iberian peninsula as tradition has it. The only historical evidence of James after Pentecost, is his end in this mortal world, described in Acts 12:1,2, where Herod Agrippa I, in an act of appeasement to Jewish outrage at the growing Christian tradition, "had James, the brother of John beheaded, and when he saw that this pleased the Jews, he went on to arrest Peter as well". Thus James, the first Apostle martyr in 44AD, fulfilled Our Lord's prophecy: "you shall drink my cup" *(Mt 20:23)*.

Saint James and Spain

If there is no hard, historical evidence that James ever preached in Spain, how is it that millions of pilgrims, over the last millennium, have made the sometime hazardous and lengthy journey - and still do - to venerate his memory at his shrine, in the most magnificent cathedral of Santiago de Compostela in the north western extremity of Spain? Tradition relates that after denial by Herod of a Christian burial, James's body was taken by his faithful disciples to the port of Jaffa, and from there underwent a miraculous voyage in a stone boat, "carried by the angels and the wind beyond the Pillars of Hercules (the Straits of Gibraltar), to land near Finisterre, at Padron, on the Atlantic coast of northern Spain". There, after subventing the trickery of the local heathen Queen Lupa, who subsequently converted to Christianity, they buried his remains inland on a hillside in Iria Flavia, at the place that was to become Santiago de Compostela. After this burial, St James's influence did not surface for another seven centuries - "the Apostle slept".

In 810AD, a hermit, Pelayo, was guided by a vision of a star to the burial place of James and two of his disciples. The discovery was reported to Theodomir, Bishop of Iria Flavia, who declared the remains as those of the Apostle. This discovery and pronouncement was taken up by Alfonso II, ruler of the small Christian kingdom which included Asturias and Galicia, which, alone on the Iberian peninsula, had thus far escaped conquest by the Moors. On the other side of the Pyrenees, the rest of European Christendom was casting a nervous eye at this last bastion of Christianity. Alfonso declared James the patron saint of Spain: a champion was awaited, and had been found.

Patron saint of Spain

Whilst a cynical twenty first century view could easily be taken of all this, there is sound literary and traditional substance that support the legend. At the location of the discovery was a typical early Christian burial site, and a martyrium, giving evidence of the cult of a saint of early patristic times. One of the derivations of Compostela is from *componere* the Latin to bury; the other, more appealing and popular, is from *campus de la stella* or *campus stellae*, the place of stars, in recognition of the bright blaze of the Milky Way, ever visible to pilgrims on a clear night, leading the way westward to Santiago. There is documentary evidence in the Martyrology of Usuard of 865 for the translation of St James's relics from Jerusalem to Spain by more conventional and gradual means.

Whilst it could be said that wistful anticipation and happy discovery followed on each other's heels, there is no denying that this discovery and authentication of the bones had the most profound effect by offering, in the first instance, compelling motivation for the Christian armies in their ensuing and long running battle against Islam in Spain. It also drew its first prominent pilgrim in 950AD - the Bishop of le Puy-en-Velay, some 900 miles away in the Haute Loire. This high profile pilgrimage gave Santiago a wide exposure to pilgrims thirsty to seek the intercession of one very near the top of the hierarchy of martyrs.

However, in 997 it looked as though the patronage as saviour of Spain was mistakenly vested in St James, because in that year the Moorish invader, Al-Mansoor, had reached and sacked Santiago itself, but reportedly fell short of destroying or desecrating the tomb. It eventually took over four centuries to rid Spain finally of the Moors. It was during this bloody process that the legend - and the inspiration of St James as the 'slayer of Moors' - *Matamoros* - came into play. The legend grew up that he appeared at four critical battles as a warrior mounted on a white horse, and inspired famous victories. So, alongside the evangelising apostle and the benevolent pilgrim, there exists the fierce warrior - the son of Thunder had truly lived up to his name.

It was at the battle of Las Navas de Tolosa in 1212 that the power of the Moors in Spain was finally broken, but it was not until 1492 that the re-conquest of Spain was complete. King Ferdinand and Queen Isabella paid homage at the tomb of St James on behalf of a grateful nation, and, one presumes an equally grateful Pontiff, although it was not until 1884 that Leo XIII declared, in his Bull *'Omnipotens Deus'*, that the remains of St James were indeed present in Santiago - something that the faithful had already known, anyway, all along.

The French also maintained an interest and influence over promoting the Way of St James, for after all, the many thousands of pilgrims traversing routes through France would contribute handsomely to local economies. The monastery at Cluny contributed to many of the religious houses on the Way, including into Spain, and the association with Charlemagne and Roland's heroic rearguard action against the ambushing Moors in the Pyrenees near Roncesvalles was heavily promoted.

Santiago, the cathedral and symbols

Meanwhile, the fortunes of Santiago continued to develop after the Moors had been rolled back southwards from Galicia. From 1000 the numbers of pilgrims started to increase, and in 1075 work started, as four independent projects, on the great Romanesque cathedral, which was consecrated in 1211. Between the ninth and thirteenth centuries Santiago grew six-fold in size.

Whilst the distinctive pilgrim garb generally started and evolved during the tenth and eleventh centuries, there is no hard evidence, other than sometime in the twelfth century, as to when the *coquille Saint Jacques* - the scallop shell - emerged and became established as the symbol of St James, and hence proud emblem of the pilgrim along his Way. The more prosaic explanation is that as these scallop shells litter the Galician beaches, they were probably collected by those pilgrims who went on to Padron and the Atlantic coast as souvenirs, and used them as an external display on their clothing to show that they had 'gone the extra mile'. The popularity of this soon caught on, and entrepreneurial locals, spotting a niche in the market, started selling them in Santiago. Subsequently the local cathedral authorities, in giving the their blessing of the scallop as St James's official emblem, claimed exclusivity and sold them on licence, thereby cornering the market.

Other, more legendary versions, tell of a horseman - depicted variously as bridegroom or local nobleman - who fell into the sea after his horse had taken fright and prayed fervently to St James to save him from drowning. The prayer was answered, and rider and horse emerged from the sea covered in scallop shells. Whatever its origins, it is a pervasive and strangely comforting and encouraging symbol seen anywhere and everywhere along the routes through Europe and on into Spain, and most importantly on just about every pilgrim on their way to and from Santiago. Possibly by happy chance the living scallop is described as being "gregarious, speedy, agile and with the ability and instinct to undertake substantial migrations".

It was not until the seventeenth and eighteenth centuries that the cathedral finally took on today's appearance, when its Romanesque features were largely hidden behind that of Baroque, in a style termed Churrigueresque after Jose Churriguera, the Spanish Michelangelo, who is credited with the final completion. In the words of one of today's explorers and travel writers, Robin Hanbury-Tenison, "The towers and cupolas scramble over each other to reach for the sky in a series of contortions which look through half closed eyes almost like the craggy rocks of a romantic landscape, or again, the ruins of a long vanished civilisation thrusting up out of the jungle".

One of the still visible and prominent Romanesque features, and so beloved of arriving pilgrims, is the elaborately carved Portico de la Gloria of 1188. Here is displayed the fine carving skills of twenty years' work of the twelfth century Master Mateo. In an action packed depiction of over 200 figures of apostles, saints and martyrs and their animals and symbols, stands the Tree of Jesse, of which, in one particular spot, millions of pilgrims' thankful touching fingers have worn away deep holes in the marble. Atop presides St James, greeting pilgrims with a benevolent and one fancies welcoming smile, and affirming his presence in Santiago with the words *Misit Me Dominus* (the Lord sent me) inscribed on a scroll in his hand.

Pilgrims arrive in Santiago

The ideal date for a pilgrim to arrive in Santiago is on the Saint's Feast day, the 25th of July, which is preceded by huge, joyful and boisterous celebrating in the city. If the Feast Day falls on a Sunday, a Holy Year is declared, and arrival on this day is the most desirable. It is only during this year that access through the *Puerta Santa*, or Holy Door, is possible for pilgrims. The door is ceremonially broken open by the Archbishop on the 31st of December preceding the Holy Year, and sealed up again at the end of the year. Inevitably Holy Years attract pilgrims in larger numbers. The figure of those being awarded their compostela for the last Holy Year, 1999, is in excess of 150,000. The next Holy Year is 2004.

Having jealously guarded his credentials or 'pilgrim passport' issued by his church or other ecclesiastical authority for the outward route - a passport that ensured his *bona fides* - the pilgrim's next goal was to obtain his *'compostela'* on arrival at Santiago. This document was issued exclusively by the cathedral authorities once they had satisfied themselves that the criteria of pilgrimage had been fulfilled. It was important, not only to secure use of pilgrim facilities on the return route, but also as proof that the destination had been satisfactorily achieved - particularly for those undergoing penitential or punishment pilgrimages, and those acting as surrogate pilgrims. Nowadays, one still has to satisfy the cathedral authorities of one's motive, and present the pilgrim passport for scrutiny. The minimum requirement in terms of distance to secure a *compostela* is to have walked no less than the last 100kms in consecutive days to Santiago, or cycled or ridden a horse for the last 200kms.

The other rituals that the pilgrim traditionally carries out on arriving in the cathedral is to pay respects to the relics housed in an ornate silver casket in the shrine under the high altar, and finally, to mount the short narrow staircase up over the high altar, where the grateful pilgrim can give the Apostle's statue a hug and a kiss. He or she will then attend the pilgrim Mass, at which if they are fortunate, the great *botafumeiro* - incense thurifer - will be swung with great ceremony towards the end.

The '*botafumeiro*' - incense thurifer

After all the hardships on the route, building up to the emotion of at last paying one's respects to St James and begging his intercession, and the holy and ultimate moment of receiving the Eucharist, it is the *botafumeiro* that provides that visual thrill and sense of theatre as a

Cathedral *tiraboleiros* prepare to swing the *botafumeiro*.

complete counterpoint to the ethereal. It is a silver incense thurifer, three quarters the height of a man and weighing nearly 80kgs. Its purpose, apart from the ritual of sending sweet smelling incense heavenward, was to blanket the odour of the hundreds of packed pilgrims in the cathedral. It requires eight men, operating an ancient rope and pulley system reaching high into the cathedral's dome, to ceremonially swing it. The spectacle of this huge, glittering object, trailing clouds of incense, swooping through the vertical before soaring dizzily to the horizontal, is enough to make even the hardened clergy watch in awe and the pilgrims to exclaim out loud in wonderment. There is also the slightly irreverent hope that, as has been reported on one past occasion, the *botafumeiro* will continue on its travel clean through one of the cathedral windows at the end of one of its majestic swings!

After these spiritual and theatrical highpoints, and as well as the joys of meeting old friends made along the Way, the pilgrim of the Middle Ages now faced probably the lowest point of his journey and the hardest test of his faith - the prospect of having to retrace his weary steps homeward.

ITER SANCTI JACOBI

A Long history

"There are four roads which, leading to Santiago, converge to form a single road at Puente la Reina, in Spanish territory". Thus starts probably the best known and one of the earliest 'guide books' to the Way of St James, the five volumed *Codex Calixtinus* written and compiled between about 1140-70. The first four volumes deal with the liturgy, miracles, glorification and history of the pilgrimage, whilst the fifth, attributed to a French cleric, provides somewhat erratic and at times bloodcurdling descriptions of places and people along the route. For instance, the Navarrese, for some reason, are singled out as being, "a barbarous nation, distinct from all other nations in habits and way and being, full of all kind of malice, and of black colour (as quoted in the English translation to *The Pilgrim's Guide* by William Melczer).

It dwells in some detail on the 'Bitter and Sweet Waters found along this Road', and warns mounted pilgrims of the poisoned waters of the Rio Salado near Lorca. The Guide goes on to detail such other things as the 'Saintly Remains on this Road' and a detailed description of 'the Church of St James' at Compostela.

Variety of Pilgrims

However, this was all a far cry for the pilgrim of the Middle Ages, more than likely illiterate, starting off on his pilgrimage, when, closing his front door for the last time, he set out south and west on his long journey. He came predominantly from France, Belgium and Germany. 'He' is used advisedly, as the only women seen travelling on the route were those few accompanying their husbands, or itinerant prostitutes. Woman were simply regarded as an unwelcome and added temptation and were thus excluded. Pilgrims also ventured from Britain, hazarding the sea crossing. Others came from Scandinavia, Eastern Europe, Italy, and a few from even further afield.

But from whatever nation they hailed, a common characteristic of the pilgrim population along the Way was its diversity: all classes and walks of life were present, from the loftiest to the lowest. The large mass, however, was made up of the humble serf or peasant - all usually at the end of their comparatively short working lives - as it was only then that they could seek release to do pilgrimage. This meant that a great majority were in poor physical condition, worn down by the hard, unremitting work and poor living standards of their times. There were also the crippled, the infirm, the handicapped, all struggling in faith and hope - and seeking charity - in their desire to reach Santiago and plead for healing. Added to these

The meeting of the Ways from Paris, Vezelay and Le Puy, with *le chemin de procession* **leading away uphill.**

were, in Professor Melczer's translation, "Truants, simulators, jesters, fools and vagrants, all so much an integral part of the scenario as the topography and the weather, the pilgrims' constant fellow travellers".

The four main routes

These individuals, or individual groups from their town or village, would gradually meet and merge with others as they all started converging on the four main continental European feeder routes that led to Spain. The most northerly and westerly is the *Via Turonense* which funnels into Paris, and then on through Orleans, Tours, Poitiers, and Bordeaux, until reaching the Spanish border. The next, the *Via Lemovicense*, gathered its pilgrims, mainly Flemish and German, at Vezelay, and took them through Bourges (or Nevers) to Limoges and Perigueux. After that is the *Via Podense*, which starts at Le Puy-en-Velay, in the Haute Loire, itself a pilgrim site. This route is the one most travelled today, passing through Conques, Figeac, Cahors, Moissac and Navarrenx. These three routes all converge at Ostabat, within sight of the Pyrenees, and so on to the frontier town of Saint-Jean-Pied-de-Port, before the pilgrim has to bend his back into the long haul up the Pyrenees to Roncesvalles, a large Augustinian monastery, the pilgrim's first Spanish experience.

Along the fourth principal route, the *Via Tolosana*, came mostly Italians and Germans, having gathered at

Arles, close to the Mediterranean, and going on through Toulouse, Auch and Oloron. It crosses the Pyrenees further to the east at the Col de Somport before it merges with the other three routes at Puenta la Reina in Spain, which now, and for the rest of the journey, is known as the *camino frances,*

There were other prominent routes. The rugged northern route that follows the Spanish coast - *the Rutas del Mar* - onto which those pilgrims from England eventually joined from la Coruna, probably with great relief, after a usually unpleasant sea voyage, making their way to Santiago along the *camino ingles*. Other British pilgrims would have made a shorter sea crossing to the Cherbourg peninsula, or to Bordeaux, and then go on to join the *Via Turonense*. Those from the south and east of Spain made their way along various established caminos, as did those from Portugal. Some pilgrims went the extra miles beyond Santiago to go to what was then regarded as the end of the known world, to the wild and storm tossed peninsula of Finisterre.

The journey

Daily progress along the Way was irregular. It was governed generally by the weather and terrain, and individually by the pilgrim's own motives and motivation. Otherwise, health and accommodation opportunities would also feature, as would time spent with, or detouring to, some favourite or popular reliquary. Some may have sought, or come upon, their own personal adventure, the saying being, "although you had to get to Compostela, you only lived once". The typical daily distances covered may have been ten miles or less for the not so fit, fifteen or so for the able and motivated, twenty and above for those sturdy folk in a hurry.

Whilst a steady trudge, accompanied sometimes by praying and singing, sometimes companionable silence was the norm, some pilgrims were seen to be going barefoot to extract maximum penitential effect, others went on their knees, others in chains and fetters. Stone carrying by pilgrims from local quarries to some ecclesiastical building site en route was not uncommon, and neatly provided the dual solutions of keeping down labour costs whilst accruing maximum penitential benefit. In all these actions there was a strong desire to imitate Christ on His via dolorosa.

Up and down the *camino* transient communities would form, with groups and even individuals coming together and walking for periods, before mutually parting from each other through different walking speeds or other requirements. Joyful reunions would be experienced up and down the route as past companions would recognise and greet each other, and none so joyful as those who finally met long lost companions at Santiago. These bondings and friendships would be formalised and perpetuated by the formation of Fraternities back in pilgrims' home towns or areas.

There was a great oral tradition and culture that built up along the Way. News would spread up and down the route with great rapidity. Gossip was the mainstay of hope, encouragement, despair. Sign language, mime and song proliferated, as those from uncommon and diverse backgrounds tried to express their common desires and thoughts.

Three great hospices along the route are described in the Guide as, "established in places they were very much needed, are holy sites, the house of God for restoring of saintly pilgrims, the resting of the needy, the consolation of the sick, the salvation of the dead, and the assistance lent to the living". To cater for the enormous numbers of pilgrims, these hospices were generally large and plentifully spread along the route. For instance in the small, typically linear town of Castrojeriz, there were at least four, some sources say seven, hospices, but of which there is little sign today. Monasteries en route are reported as being particularly diligent in dispensing Christian hospitality, "never knowing whether the next wayfarer was humble pilgrim or Christ himself".

'Pilgrims of the world'

The coursing pulse of these great arteries that lead across Europe to the pilgrim's heart in Santiago de Compostela may have diminished to a weak flutter over the past three hundred years or so, but there are signs in the latter part of the twentieth century that the beat is picking up again. Although structured religion may be under assault, there are still many people searching for the spiritual, the undefined, and pilgrimage in many instances meets this urge. The possibilities of international travel by air, combined with an increasingly raised awareness in many parts of the world of the existence of Santiago, is bringing in pilgrims from countries completely beyond the ken of the Middle Ages: Brazil, USA, Australia, South Africa.

As indicated earlier, numbers along the camino are rising significantly. The wisdom of history has shown us the effects of abuse and exploitation of pilgrims and pilgrimage. Today's traditional 'journeying' pilgrims, whether on foot, bicycle or horseback, should be afforded every encouragement along their way, and not be regarded just as a commercial proposition. Those who travel direct to Santiago, or any pilgrim site, as a tourist - the curiositas of yesteryear - should also be accorded the same welcome and respect, for in the Holy Father's words, they, "are also pilgrims of the world" , and, "it is also necessary for tourism and commercial agents not to be dominated only by economic interests, but also to be aware of their human and social functions". Guardians of the Ways of St James take heed.

The Cathedral of Santiago de Compostela.

Accommodation

Accommodation along the GR can be as varied as can the pilgrim's pocket be deep - from best hotel, to humble *gîtes d'étape*. Most pilgrims tend to stay in the gîtes, for this is where the pilgrim spirit is generated, rubbing shoulders with fellow pilgrims in humble, often spartan, but convivial surroundings. As in the Middle Ages, the gites came in all shapes and styles, and were provided by various organisations:

14th April. "Waited for Tourist Office to open and booked into municipal gites which is grotty, compared to what I have been used to so far - do me good! Shared tiny, stuffy, four bedded bunk room with married French couple - some more snoring." (I still keep in touch with this couple, from Paris.)

Some gites were privately run, this one in a farm house:

16th April. "As I write, my peace and quiet in this part of the gites (I was by myself in a six bedded *dortoire* (dormitory) in which I smugly thought I would be the sole occupant) is somewhat shattered by the arrival of a French family, Mum, Dad and three children with whom I'll be sharing my dorm - very interesting!... Uneventful night with 'my' family - quite nostalgic to hear the gentle breathing of children asleep, along with child noises in the night." There was a definite humbling process under-way here, which I recognised, welcomed, and tried to take on board.

Other gîtes were run by devoted lay people who give their lives to tending to pilgrims' needs, such as the two families who run, with no income other than pilgrim donations, *Hospitalité St Jacques*. This tasteful, welcoming and holy establishment, in an old diocesan house in Estaing, fed our bodies and spirits:

19th April. "1600 pilgrims passed through here last year - their family lives can never be their own - they have my greatest admiration". Of course, they see their 'family' as those hundreds of pilgrims to whom they lovingly tend every year.

In the tradition of the Way there was the occasional accommodation opportunity in a monastery or convent. I had the privilege of spending Easter at Conques, a small well preserved medieval town with the beautiful Romanesque Abbey church of Ste Foy (St Faith). The guest wing consisted of large airy *dortoires*, the popularity of which was evident from the profusion of rather wobbly three tiered metal bunks! Or the convent at Vaylats slightly off the route, but well worth the detour, as the nuns lovingly lavished their hospitality on us:

26th April. "Just time to unpack, wash, shave, do washing - go to evening prayer, and then feast of an evening meal - soup, bean salad, spaghetti with bacon, cheese, coffee, pudding. Lashings of wine. Totally spoilt with single room, basin, all for 10 francs - can't cope!"

There was the rare and unexpected treat that even impressed my French fellow pilgrims of *'la France profonde'* when we stayed at a private, very rural gîtes at St Antoine:

2nd May: "Supper an absolute riot - very 'deep France' - *'Le Patron'* - a 72 year old working farmer held court. Cap on back of head, wicked twinkle, ferocious knife for slicing and gesticulating. Wine kept flowing, everyone in high spirits."

Joy of companionship

By this time I was summing up my fellow travellers. They were mainly French, although my diary notes on *16th April:* "Met up with Terje my Norwegian chum from the first night (we are still in touch) and also met two Brits en route". Later on I noted that the Dutch couple I encountered were, "a retired banker, and his wife, a Protestant pastor, who both spoke perfect English and French. It turns out that Ben, the husband, had done National Service in the Rhodesian Rifles!" (my own background being from Africa, but I had learned by now that this pilgrimage was producing no end of amazing and unexpected surprises).

I was also learning not to bat an eyelid at the mixed sleeping and domestic arrangements in the gites, as to everyone else it all seemed totally normal:

"Sharing dorm with noisy group of French ladies, one of them, although small in stature, snored for France - all night! Glad to escape at 0630."

From my fellow travellers I experienced nothing but consideration and courtesy; the French were proud of their country and eager to display this; they were very tolerant of my language limitations and made every effort to include me in the proceedings. I experienced nothing approaching the avaricious inn keepers and traders reported by the pilgrim of the Middle Ages. Whilst our small travelling community did not display the colourful and wide spread of the classes of the Middle Ages, it more than compensated with the ever growing international make-up of the pilgrims and a wide age range. In the time honoured tradition, news of one's fellow pilgrims travelled up and down the route with great rapidity.

One of the greatest joys was being totally away from the tourist routes and attractions that can so blight a nation's true identity. On the pilgrim route one was completely in amongst, and part of, the fabric of daily life going on around:

28th April, rest day at Cahors: "I love being in amongst the real French and their daily lives; whilst not being able to fully participate I am very happy to spectate. I am writing this in a lovely old library surrounded by ancient books. I was allowed to stay (it was not generally open to the public) by pleading the ignorant *'anglais pèlerin'* to an obliging librarian."

Through France to the Pyrenees

Progress in France averaged about 15 miles per day, although daily distances did vary according to accommodation availability. After the initial snows of the Massif Central, the spring weather held, and my diary records most days as "gloriously sunny". Walking as an individual afforded the luxury of going entirely at one's own pace, without having the worry of inconveniencing anybody else. It was quite acceptable to join other pilgrims, often complete strangers, for a spot of companionship, and no one took offence if you felt the desire to peel off and seek solitude:

13th May. " I felt really blessed today. Most glorious weather - blue sky, sunshine, stunning scenery with the Pyrenees always in the background. Came across four French mountain bikers, whom I had joked with earlier. They were obviously praying, looking out over what must be close to Paradise. I joined them and listened to Psalm 149 - a very special moment for me. Photo taken, address given - I hope to see the end result. (I did.) Whole experience cheered me no end - again thanks to the Lord for this marvellous encounter."

Churches, chapels, shrines, and wayside crucifixes were generally in abundance along the Way: "Stopped at the *Chapelle de Bastide* - gorgeous little chapel - not even with a proper door, just a wicket gate." Many of the small chapels had a pilgrim book in which to write messages of gratitude and encouragement. Peace, utter peace and tranquillity, a complete feeling of calm and serenity, reigned supreme in these holy places. However big or small, grand or humble, a summary over which one could reflect when sitting in them could not have been better put by a Georges Dubuy of the French Academy writing about Conques Abbey in 1994:

"Medieval man could not imagine a barrier between the visible universe and the next world. The Abbey Church at Conques was thus conceived as a place where God and man could meet, or as a gateway. This Church should be viewed as a sort of ante room to Paradise, an imperfect copy of the Heavenly Jerusalem, and we should at the same time bear in mind that the harmonies of its inner spaces were planned to evoke a premonitory vision of timeless perfection."

Never eating alone

Feeding was a relatively simple affair. In a town or a village, the French in their own civilised way, open their cafes and bars, it seems, at a very early hour of the day. A large cup of hot chocolat and a croissant was a perfect start to the day. If this was not available, one had to have the foresight to buy an apple and bar of chocolate and eat these at the gites, with a cup of strong, self brewed black coffee, before setting off at six thirty, or by the latest seven o'clock, into a usually glorious morning. As the route generally kept away from civilisation during the day, again one would have to buy fruit, cheese, meat and pick one's private picnic spot somewhere with a commanding view.

Most gîtes in France have some form of self catering kitchen, and many pilgrims, particularly the French, took great pride in cooking up delicious meals. Generally, I made up the 'away team', and ate out if there was a restaurant nearby. On these occasions I never ate alone - sometimes groups of complete strangers would invite me to join them. Some gîtes included an evening meal, which were plentiful and wholesome, and with the amount of energy expended during the day, there was no feelings of guilt over the huge quantities of food appreciatively put away.

14th May. "Ostabat to St-Jean-Pied-de-Port, 20 kilometres, 0715-1315. Another lovely day. Not the best of day's walking, route not inspiring and knee giving trouble and worry. Last three quarters of a kilometre hard work".

St-Jean-Pied-de-Port is as good as half way from le Puy to Santiago, and it is here that I had to rest for three days to have my creaky knee attended to, and take stock of my situation as I contemplated the next 450 miles:

14th May: "All in all feeling rather gloomy at prospects of going on, let alone completing. But whatever, I am content to let the Lord take me as far as He thinks I need to go".

El Camino de Santiago

Facing the Pyrenees

The pilgrim, having gathered his physical and spiritual strength and resolve in St-Jean-Pied-de-Port, now looks up at the Pyrenees, and contemplates the next stage of the journey. Having mastered and enjoyed the familiarity of the routine and the journey through France, thoughts now turn to Spain, and the differences it will hold. It is here also, that the majority of modern pilgrims come to start their pilgrimage to Santiago. Those 'old hands' from le Puy and other destinations, whilst watching with some amusement (and possible air of superiority?) the enthusiasm and excitement of those joining, start to get an inkling of the true internationalism gathering to walk along this ancient pilgrim route, and that French will no longer be the predominant language of the Way:

17th May. "Gîtes (in St Jean) full, with interesting mix: Brazilians, South African and New Zealander, Brit, French and a Pole. Usual cacophony of snoring, its good to be back in the routine!"

Into Spain

For the *Via Podensis*, the GR 65, now gives way to the *camino frances*, or more commonly the *Camino de*

Santiago. It is no longer primarily a recreational walker's route: it is a pilgrim route, designed to transport the pilgrim in a workmanlike manner as swiftly and as effortlessly as possible to their destination. The waymark signs, are no longer the neat, discreet *balises* of France, but the more blatant, and not so artistic, yellow arrows *(flechas)*. The camino faithfully follows the pilgrim route almost exactly - no unnecessary detours to admire the scenery. In some places it runs beside the main road, and for some of the way it is a custom built pedestrian track - soon dubbed the camino 'super high way'.

18th May. "St Jean to Roncesvalles, 26 kilometres, 0730-1530. Up hill all day... knee very understanding, complaining a bit at the end, but gives me hope at least for tomorrow. Abbey in remote spot... gorgeous collegiate Church". I was on my way again.

Accommodation

The range of accommodation along the camino still offers the many options of France, from the smart hotel downwards. However, the simple pilgrim accommodation now took on a completely different characteristic. One now looked for the refugio or albergues - still physically a hostel, still varying in standards of comfort and cleanliness, still provided by a variety of agencies, but most were nominally 'free', depending entirely on pilgrim donations (usually 300 pesetas a day), for income. They also increased in

frequency along the route, catering for the increased numbers, but also allowing more flexibility for daily progress.

20th May. "Refugio in Pamplona above church in city
centre. Clean, well modernised, efficient, friendly reception, usual crowded dorm… There followed the noisiest
night ever - Pamplona was in all-night party mode, and
the noise of shouting, singing, drums, bugles, laughter,
just did not abate all night!"

Although this was an exception (it was Saturday
night), it gave us a clue that life was going to be different
in Spain. The days were geared to a much later start in the
morning for shops and businesses; everything came to a
halt at midday for the afternoon siesta, and sluggishly
came-to in the early evening, with life picking up again
later at night. Some refugios did not open until a given
time in the afternoon:

22nd May. "Had to wait with others for refugio to open -
very pleasant and jovial sitting in the warm sunshine. 'Five
star' refugio, very well managed with care and pride."

Some refugios, in the tradition of the Middle Ages,
were run by volunteer *hospitaleros* drawn from all the
pilgrim nationalities:

26th May. "Refugio (at Granon) is an absolute gem in a
beautifully restored and adapted bell tower. Small dorm on
mezzanine floor (on mats) above lovely large
communal/dining area and good facilities all round. Very
welcoming Belgian *hospitalero* who also cooked supper.

Mass in church below - large congregation, mostly of the 'mamas'. Had the most stupendous supper - my contribution being the washing up".

Others, provided by the local community, were very basic indeed:

27th May. "The small town is in bad order - main road thundering through it - no renewal or maintenance of anything anywhere. Refugio in old, disused school building - very basic, one shower, two squat loos, but at least beds, can't and not grumbling at 125 pesetas a night - but what a contrast from last night!" (the bell tower at Granon). By now I was no longer surprised, and even took delight in the contrasts, twists, turns and surprises that the camino produced on a daily basis.

Pilgrim numbers swelling

The closer one got to Santiago, the more it was obvious that pilgrimaging was being taken very seriously. In Ponferrada, with 125 miles to go, was a brand new, large custom built, privately donated refugio, "with 4 person bunk rooms, large dining reception area, superb washing and toilet facilities". Once into Galicia, all the refugios were provided by the local authority, were mostly newly built, comfortable, and in a standard pattern, which soon became recognisable along the route.

Pilgrims on the route were now plentiful; the Spanish contingent swelled considerably day by day, the closer we got to Santiago. With an enforced three day rest at St Jean, I had lost a lot of my old chums from the French leg, although I started catching up with some along the latter part of the camino and in Santiago, and this was one of the great joys, being re-united with friends. The other is making new friends, many of which have made an indelible impression on my memory.

Through country and city

Progress in Spain averaged about 16 miles a day. Although there was the odd mountain range to get over and hill to climb, the going was generally firm underfoot and level of gradient in comparison to GR 65. The wide horizons were ever present when tramping across the *meseta* - miles and miles, and days and days of wheat fields, with hardly a sign of habitation in sight:

31st May. "Steady climb up onto the *meseta*, along the endless track through endless wheatfields - everywhere lush and green, poppies providing brave scarlet splashes."

Where habitation did meet the wheat fields, the long straight stretches invariably headed for grain silos in the distant town, and for however long one walked, they never seemed to get nearer! The weather again mainly stayed fair during the Spanish leg; late spring / early summer seemed a good option, although it was probably by luck rather than judgement that the weather stayed so sunny in Galicia, not normally noted for long dry spells.

Because the route generally went through towns and cities, one had to endure some urban eyesores and smells, such as industrial estates, municipal tips, building sites and traffic-ridden town approaches like that into Burgos on seven kilometres of seemingly never ending pavements, and Leon where, "the approach was pretty hideous along hard shoulder of fast road". Spotting the *flechas* in busy towns also became an art form, as again in Leon, "had slight problems finding convent in middle of town". The rewards, however were usually abundant in the form of the cathedrals, such as that in Leon, where I noted "a big 'wow' factor with huge and many stained glass windows", and not long after that, the joys of abundant bars and cafes for "beer and tortilla". Some good souls along the way attempted to alleviate the urban eyesores: on the approach into the town of Najera, was painted a stirring pilgrim poem in Castillian on a factory wall (referred to in the opening section).

Mass along the way

Gone now were the little chapels experienced in France. It was now mainly working parish churches in the towns and villages, many of which were locked. However, the upside, which was not the case in France, was access to a church service - invariably Mass - just about every evening. Although these timings seemed to be for the benefit of the pilgrim, congregations were also full with parishioners, and not always just the stereotyped 'mamas' in black. This bonus started to heighten one's spiritual build up for Santiago; there were also many pilgrim blessings given at these Masses, which made one feel a bit special, and at a couple of small services held after Mass, the names and nationalities of those pilgrims who had expected to arrive at Santiago on that day were read out and prayed for, as I knew mine would on my expected arrival date.

There was also plenty of evidence, either showing physically or indicated verbally by the guide book, of the great Hospitals and monasteries that once proudly and prominently stood along the Way. Standing by the ruins, in the tranquillity of the day, it did not take great imagination, or even sensitivity, to hear the echoes of ancient times, to hear the babble of those crowds of pilgrims, the stench, the dust; to feel the friendly and strangely comforting aura of the ghosts of those who tended the hundreds of thousands of peregrinos who passed that way, those many hundreds of years ago. In contrast, there is a delightful display of ongoing hospitality where, opposite one of the first Benedictine houses in Navarra, an enterprising *bodega* (wine grower and merchant) has provided a wine fountain where the thirsty pilgrim is invited to partake, but not to abuse ("Caution on a hot day...", the guide book advises!). It would appear that either the Navarrese have improved their ways tremendously since the original Guide was written, or that their description as being a "barbarous nation" was just a touch more than French disdain from the author.

Pilgrim cairns

One of the smaller curiosities along all the Way was the custom of piling and balancing stones and pebbles upon each other, creating small and large cairns in or on all sorts of improbable surfaces. Apparently these *humiliatorios* or *milladoiros* were created by passing pilgrims in an echo of pagan days when the tossing of a stone on to a cairn would invoke the deities that offered protection to travellers. These cairns therefore balance precariously on concrete milestones or stone crosses. In one spot along the camino, obviously a resting place for pilgrims, is a profusion of these small cairns, giving the impression of a fertile field of some strange, petrified crop.

The most celebrated cairn, one which can take a good climbing on, and some 140 miles from Santiago, is the Cruz de Ferro, a large iron cross atop a mountain near the highest point of the camino. Intended as a navigation mark, pilgrims now traditionally deposit a stone, usually carried from their home, as symbolic of dumping their sins, before moving on to Santiago, with clear conscience and fresh resolve. It was intriguing to see other pilgrims' offerings; mine was an ugly, jagged, man-made affair of concrete and pebble, where "the highlight of the day was depositing my horrible rock as symbolic of ridding myself of my past sins and dedicating myself anew to a Christian life".

The arrangements for feeding had also changed on departure from France. Gone were the early opening cafes, so an apple to start the day usually sufficed; however, elevenses was keenly anticipated, as that usually meant a very tasty tortilla and a large, deliciously milky coffee. The refugios generally did not have kitchens, if so, they were small and basic. Compared with France, eating out was a disappointment, mainly I suspect, because in the lower price-range restaurants in which we chose to eat, it was very hit and miss affair, invariably having to select one's meal from the verbal menu rattled off in Spanish, by a usually very amused waitress.

Approaching the Mount of Joy

The relativity of our daily modest rate of progress only became really apparent some 120 miles from Santiago, when walking beside the main road which led to Santiago, one of my fellow pilgrims commented, "those cars will be in Santiago in three or four hours. For us, it will be another eight or so days". Up until now I had never taken it for granted that I would actually get to Santiago - another major lesson of the Way, until:

11th June at Eirexe. "With only 45 or so miles to go, I actually feel quite overwhelmed at my impending arrival at Santiago, now a probability and actuality rather than just a plan and an aim. My whole pilgrimage, starting at le Puy, those long weeks ago, has just reeled past me in a great wave of recollection and emotion."

Monte del Gozo (Mount of Joy) is a highly significant place on the camino. It is the feature that after the pilgrim crests, he sees the city of Santiago de Compostela for the first time, some three miles away. For the Pope's visit in 1989 it was turned into a huge open area for Mass, with below it, a large modern complex of accommodation for students, holiday makers and pilgrims. Many pilgrims rest here before making the final, joyful approach into Santiago, next morning, fresh, and in time for the midday pilgrim Mass at the Cathedral.

14th June. Monte del Gozo to Santiago, 0830-1000, three miles. "Unusual experience of no-one rustling around at 0530. Novelty of getting up in broad daylight, and not having to connive when to dive into the loo to beat the rush! Went up the hill on this glorious morning to the pilgrim statues that point joyfully to the Cathedral - what a lovely sight - the triple towers clearly visible in the bright morning sun. Breakfast at 0800 and then set off down the hill at a luxuriant amble, savouring every minute. Lost the signs to the Cathedral… and then, suddenly, the first glimpse, the statue of St James above a door, and then round the corner to that most glorious front façade. At that time of morning the large square was quite empty. Mixed feeling of great joy but also anticlimax, not quite sure what to do next..."

This mood did not last long, for I had various things that every pilgrim over the centuries has had to accomplish on arrival in Santiago. I sought out the nearby Cathedral compostela office. There I presented my well stamped Pilgrim Passport proving passage from le Puy. After a few gentle questions about my motives for my pilgrimage, I was presented with my compostela, an impressive Latin document made out to 'Dnum. Davidem Baldwin'. Then, having found a bed for the night, I returned to the Cathedral for the midday pilgrim Mass. There I had a "joyful reunion with Bernard and Remy whom I had met on Day 2", with whom, even at this late stage, I had now finally caught up after separating in France, those many weeks ago. Mass was a crowded, jubilant affair, to a cathedral packed mainly with tourists, but pilgrims were also well in evidence. My diary records, "I did my best to concentrate and give thanks properly", but it was difficult with all the hubbub and the distractions; the swinging of the *botafumeiro* was spectacular, and yes, that little mischievous part of my mind did for a fleeting moment gleefully envisage it swinging on clean through the window.

Needless to say, there were celebrations of a more secular nature that evening with my fellow pilgrims, but they were quietly reminiscent and reflective. I saved my private and deepest thanks for the next day, when my excitement had subsided, and I had had time to reflect on my circumstance as 'an arrived pilgrim'. With a deep sense of fulfilment I completed the pilgrim ritual: I prayed at the shrine of St James, I gave his magnificent statue above the high altar a hug and a kiss, I pressed my fingers, feeling those worn holes, into the Tree of Jesse. I went to Mass again, where I was now able to concentrate fully. I was truly, in George Dubuy's words quoted earlier, "in the ante room of Paradise".

The strange thing was, having completed those pilgrim routines and no longer feeling the weight of my pack on my back as I wandered round Santiago sightseeing, I now realised that I was no longer a pilgrim - this journey at least, was over - it was time to return home. My thoughts turned with admiration and respect to my counterparts of the Middle Ages who would now have faced the lengthy and hazardous return journey to their front doors many, many miles and footsore steps away. They had yet to safely complete their pilgrimage - as, in the broadest sense, have we all.

"There is no permanent city for us here; we are looking for the one that is yet to be". *(Heb 13:14)*

PILGRIMAGE REFLECTIONS AND DEVOTIONS

"Lived as a celebration of one's own faith, for the Christian, a pilgrimage is a manifestation of worship to be accomplished faithfully according to tradition, with an intense religious sentiment and as a fulfilment of paschal existence.

The very dynamics of pilgrimages clearly reveals some steps that pilgrims take. They become a paradigm of the whole life of faith; *departure* reveals the decision of pilgrims to go forward up to the destination and achieve the spiritual objectives of their baptismal vocation; *walking* leads them to solidarity with their brothers and sisters and to the necessary preparation for the meeting with the Lord; the *visit to the shrine* invites them to listen to the Word of God and to sacramental celebration; *the return*, in the end, reminds them of their mission in the world as witness of salvation and builders of peace".
(The Pilgrimage in the Great Jubilee)

DEPARTURE

Chose and read some of the following:

    Gn 12:1-9 Abraham's departure.

    Ps 25 'For my hope is in you all day long'.

    Ex 33:12-17 'I myself shall go with you'.

    Heb 11:8-10 Abraham's faith.

    Jn 14:1-4 Jesus goes ahead.

Thomas Merton, A Prayer

My Lord God
    I have no idea where I am going
I do not see the road ahead of me.
I cannot know for certain where it will end.
    Nor do I really know myself,
    and the fact that I think I am following
    your will does not mean
    that I am actually doing so.
But I believe that my desire to please you
    does in fact please you.
    And I hope that I have that desire
    in all that I am doing.
    I hope that I will never do anything
    apart from that desire.
And I know that if I do this
    you will lead me by the right road
    though I may know nothing about it.
Therefore will I trust you always
    though I may seem to be lost
    and in the shadow of death.
I will not fear,
    for you are ever with me,
    and you will never leave me
    to face my perils alone.

'As you went with Joseph'

O God, our own God, true and living Way; as you went with your servant Joseph on his travels, so, Master, guide this your servant on his present journey. Protect him against trying circumstances, bad weather and every stratagem that may be directed against his welfare. Give him peace and strength; grant him the prudence he needs if he is to act as he ought, in accordance with your commandments. Bring him back home rich in the goods of this world and in heaven's blessings. For kingship, power and glory are yours, Father, Son and Holy Spirit, now and always, age after age. Amen. *(Walter Mitchell, Early Christian Prayer)*

Without the Way,
there is no going;
without the Truth,
there is no knowing;
without the Life,
there is no living.
(Thomas à Kempis, The Imitation of Christ)

Selflessness

I prayed with my family before setting off, as no doubt did the pilgrim of the Middle Ages. Whilst the hazards I faced along the route were minimal, I was not so confident as to how I would regard and relate to my fellow pilgrims - after all, I am typically stiff-upper-lip and riddled with all the prejudices of the English with regard to foreigners and all things foreign. The fact that I would be living cheek-by-jowl in the gîtes and pilgrim refuges in really quite intimate conditions, with not only strangers of both sexes, but foreigners to boot, was a source of slightly morbid fascination to me. The gloomy prediction from my guidebook to "expect no-one, repeat no-one, along the route to speak or understand English" added to my sense of foreboding. "Please, Lord, help me be nice to people that I know I am not going to like", was my simple but rather confused plea.

As soon as I set off along the Way I quickly observed that this hugger-mugger way of life seemed to be perfectly natural and acceptable to my fellow travellers, and this helped me to take it all in my stride, rapidly breaking down any sense of reserve or self consciousness. It also became obvious early on that consideration for others was a major factor (with the exception of snoring, but that was accepted by most as an unfortunate but inevitable act of nature, and was usually a subject of (albeit black) humour rather than rancour!). I personally experienced nothing but courtesy and selflessness from my fellow pilgrims, and witnessed many acts of kindness along the way.

The other thing that I discovered was the strong sense of companionship that existed almost by default. Although we were all from different countries and backgrounds, we were all sharing a quite unique and uncommon experience.

And to communicate this we found no limit to our language abilities through smile, gesture and extravagant mime when required! This extraordinary breaking down of barriers was both heart-warming and revealing - in fact I do not think the barriers even existed in the first place. I now often wonder what the effect would be if all politicians were required to undergo the Way of St James - together. I am sure the world would be a more understanding and forgiving place if they half sorted themselves out in the calm and considerate manner that we did.

Conditions became more cramped and crowded as the Way progressed, but this only served to increase the 'selfless factor'. Dormitories became more congested, and mixed showering took on an art form of discretion, involving split second timing of opening cubicle doors and positioning of towels! But we were all seasoned campaigners by now, and our goal was in sight.

My only hope is that I succeeded in stifling all that I could of my own selfishness to give back to my fellow pilgrims as good as they gave me and others - I know their example certainly inspired me to try my best. My biggest challenge now is to carry across this desire and implement it in the world that I have come back to - where the barriers are big and ugly.

"How wonderful it is, how pleasant, for God's people to live together in harmony!" *(Ps 133:1)*

WALKING

Songs of Ascents

Chose and read from among *Ps 120-134*:
These are the Songs of Ascents, sung by the people as
they went up to the Temple in Jerusalem.

> We are a people that is walking,
> and walking together we want to reach
> a city that will never end,
> without pain or sadness,
> city of eternity
> *(Latin American song)*

A merciful God

One of the other questions that comes my way when
people envisage those long lonely stretches each day, is
what exactly did I think about, and did I get bored? The
answer to the second question is definitely not. At the
very least there was so much to look at, listen to and
sniff at. All the natural sounds and smells from which
the modern world insulates us, announced their presence
in no uncertain terms.

This - all part of God's marvellous Creation - provided an over abundance of riches, which I tried not to
get too blasé about, remembering to thank God for not
only allowing me the privilege of being there, but for

displaying it in all its glory. The other trick I learned was frequently to turn and look backwards - the retreating views were just as good as they were ahead - and it would, after all, save me having to make the return trip!

As to what I thought about - well, the opportunity for reflection, meditation and prayer was great. Some of the time my mind would be in freewheel, slowly turning over and then latching onto a subject - maybe an aspect of one's past life, maybe thoughts for the future, maybe pondering a specific subject. Much of the time this process was unstructured, because again, I realised that I had the luxury of not having to rush it, in the way we normally have to, in what Newman describes as "the fever of our lives". If I had not resolved a matter, I could put it aside and come back to it at another time.

An important part of this process for me was the full realisation that although you could fool anyone at any or all the time, including yourself if you wanted, you certainly could not fool God. So it was a time to open fully to Him - in the words of Cardinal Hume - "whispering into the ear of a merciful and compassionate God the story of my life I have never been able to tell anyone".

Being admonished to return to myself I entered into my own depths, with You as guide, and I was able to do it because You were my helper. *(St Augustine)*

Chant des pèlerins de Compostelle

(The Song of the Compostela Pilgrims, in current use)
Tous les matins, nous prenons le chemin,
Every morning we set off along the way,
Tous les matins, nous allons plus loin,
Every morning, we go a little further,
Jours après jours, la route nous appelle,
Day after day, the road beckons us,
C'est la voix de Compostelle.
It is the call of Compostela.

Ultreia, Ultreia. *Onward, Onward.*
Et sus eia. *Take courage.*
Deus, adjuvanos! *God help us!*

Chemin de terre et chemin de foi,
Way of earth and way of faith,
Voie millenaire de l'Europe,
Millennium way of Europe,
La voie lactée de Charlemagne,
The Milky Way of Charlemagne,
C'est le chemin de tous les jacquets.
The way of all James's pilgrims.

Et tout là-bas au bout du continent,
And down there at the edge of the land,
Messire Jacques nous attend,
My lord James awaits us,

Depuis toujours son sourire fixe,
His smile is fixed for ever,
Le soleil qui meurt au Finistere.
As the sun dies off Finisterre.

The face of God

One of many questions I am asked is whether the pilgrimage has changed me. The flippant answer is that I have lost over a stone in weight, and two inches off my waist. However, this was only an obliging by-product. The main purpose for my journey was spiritual. I saw it as a profession of faith, with elements of thanksgiving and atonement, and a fresh commitment to Christian life. It was also an opportunity for me to plumb the depths of my spirit.

I was also hoping, probably somewhat naively and over-piously, that by putting myself in such a concentrated period of meditation, prayer and commitment of spirit, I would somehow earn the special privilege of meeting God face to face. I earnestly wondered and marvelled at how this would manifest itself - unlikely to be some Pauline experience, of course, but possibly one of honoured revelation or small manifestation.

In fact, the simple answer was, and had been, all around me all the time - and that realisation did eventually hit me with the force of revelation. He was there every day, firstly shining from His most glorious Creation through which I was passing daily: the song of nightingales, the cathedral-like forests, the non-stop display of wild flowers in their miniature perfection, the Pyrenees in their huge and majestic glory.

Most tellingly though, His face shone constantly from the people I met on the way, from the simple and small acts of kindness, courtesy, and good will, which were all in abundance from pilgrims and others en route, to those who dedicated themselves to looking after pilgrims. There was the Spanish man, who gave up his evenings to undertake the humble task of tending to pilgrims' battered feet - it was also, I have to say, quite a spectator sport! There were the two families at Estaing who give their lives giving succour to passing pilgrims; there was the simple, spontaneous and holy moment when I joined the young French mountain bikers on a hilltop and prayed Psalm 149 against a Pyrenean backdrop.

To many readers this simple realisation may smack of what in the Armed Services we jokingly called 'stating the obvious with confidence' - but up until then I had been blind to this. So, to my fellow myopics I offer, in hope, the chance of a clearer view; and to the rest of you, in humility, that no matter how short your journey is today or any other day, at least a reminder to keep a look out for God's face from among those you encounter. You may even be moved to reflect His face onto others through what you say and do.

Earth is crammed with heaven and every
  common bush on fire with God.
But only he who sees takes off his shoes,
  the rest sit and pluck blackberries.
  (Elizabeth Barrett Browning)

Trust wholeheartedly in Yahweh,
Put no faith in your own perception
Acknowledge him in every course you take,
And he will see that your paths are smooth. *(Pr 3:5,6)*

VISIT TO THE SHRINE

Chose and read some of the following:
  Ps 24 'For a solemn entry into the sanctuary'.
  Is 60:4-6 The splendour of Jerusalem
  Mt 2:1-12 The visit of the Magi.

  "...You are not here to verify,
  Instruct yourself, or inform curiosity
  Or carry report.
  You are here to kneel
  Where prayer has been valid".
  (T S Eliot Collected Poems 1966)

The pilgrimage of the Christian today

"The aim, towards which the pilgrim's itinerary is directed, is first of all the tent of meeting with God. Isaiah
already mentioned these words of God: 'My house will
be called a house of prayer for all peoples.' *(Is 56:7)*

"Pilgrimages lead to the tent of meeting with the Word of God. The fundamental experience of the pilgrim must be that of listening because 'the word of Yahweh (will go out) from Jerusalem' *(Is 2:3)*. Thus, the primary commitment of the holy journey is that of evangelisation which is often ingrained in the holy places themselves. The proclamation, reading and meditation of the Gospel must accompany the steps of the pilgrim and the visit to the shrine itself, so that what the Psalmist affirmed may be accomplished: 'Your word is a lamp to my feet, a light on my path'. *(Ps 119:105)*

"Pilgrimages also lead to the tent of the meeting with the Church, 'assembly of those who are called together by the Word of God to form the People of God. Being nourished by the body of Christ, they themselves form the Body of Christ'. *(CCC n. 777)*

"The shrine is also the tent of meeting in reconciliation. There, in fact, the pilgrim's conscience is moved; there he confesses his sins; there he is forgiven and forgives; there he becomes a new creature through the sacrament of reconciliation; there he experiences divine mercy and grace.

"The goal of pilgrimages must be the tent of the Eucharistic meeting with Christ. If the Bible is the book of pilgrims par excellence, the Eucharist is the bread that sustains them on their way, as it was for Elijah on his ascent to Horeb. *(Cf. 1K 19:4-8)*

"Pilgrimages may also be the tent of meeting with charity. A charity that is first of all that of God who loved us first by sending his Son into the world. This love is not manifested only in Christ's gift as a victim of expiation for our sins *(Cf. 1 Jn 4:10)* but also in the miraculous signs that heal and console, as Christ himself did during his earthly pilgrimage, and which are still repeated in the history of shrines.

"Pilgrimages also lead to the tent of meeting with humankind. All the religions of the world have their own holy itineraries and their holy cities. In every place of the earth, God himself becomes a meeting with the pilgrim and proclaims a universal convocation to participate fully in the joy of Abraham. In particular, the three great monotheistic religions are called to find again 'the tent of meeting' in the faith so that they may witness and build messianic justice and peace before all peoples, to redeem history.

"Pilgrimages also have as their goal the tent of personal meeting with God and with oneself. Lost in the multiplicity of daily anxieties and realities, people need to discover themselves through reflection, meditation, prayer, an examination of conscience, silence.

"While persons are on pilgrimage they also have the chance to enter the tent of cosmic meeting with God. Shrines are often located in places with an extraordinary panorama; they manifest greatly fascinating artistic forms; they concentrate in themselves ancient historical memories; they are expressions of popular and refined culture. It is therefore necessary for pilgrimages not to exclude this dimension of the spirit.

"Finally, pilgrimages are very often the way to enter the tent of meeting with Mary, the Mother of the Lord. Mary, in whom the pilgrimage of the Word towards humankind converges with humankind's pilgrimage of faith, is 'the one who advanced on the pilgrimage of faith, thus becoming the 'star of evangelisation' for the journey of the whole Church... Her womb was the first shrine, the tent of meeting between divinity and humanity... The Magnificat then becomes the song par excellence, not only of the peregrinatio Mariae, but also of our pilgrimage in hope." *(The Pilgrimage in the Great Jubilee)*

Jesu! All praise to Thee,
Our joy and endless rest!
Be thou our guide while pilgrims here
Our crown amid the blest.
(Anon: Saevo dolorum turbine)

Footprints

One of the great practical and tangible forces that drove me during my pilgrimage were footprints. They were constantly in front of me all along the Way. I knew that they belonged to pilgrims who were either just a bit further on, or maybe a day or two ahead. I also knew that whatever conditions I was enduring - bad (or good) weather, injury, difficult terrain, lovely views - that I was not alone; those ahead of me were experiencing much the same, as were those who followed. This thought was both comforting and encouraging.

Whenever I got temporarily lost my first resort was to search for the footprints. If there were few or none on the track I knew I was definitely off course, and I would cast back to where they took up the trail again. I only had one slight scare, and that was when I was obviously the first person going through extensive woodland after a fresh snowfall. The waymarking was 'iffy', there were numerous other trails through the woods, and the most well worn was not obvious beneath the blanket of snow. In fact at one stage I turned and looked back and saw the sobering evidence of only one set of prints, which led right up to me. Thankfully, my visions of a frost bitten, half-starved pilgrim blundering around a wood somewhere in France, did not materialise!

However, the closer one got to Santiago, the more obvious and defined the camino became, not only by the increasing number of people visible on the route, but for long stretches it was a purpose built pilgrim track. This definition further increased with the appearance of marker stones every 500 yards or so from some 100 miles out of Santiago, and on which was the familiar coquille (escalope shell).

But these were all indications of the present. What was of the greatest, and continuing inspiration for me, is of those millions of now invisible footprints that preceded me over the last thousand years, and of those that no doubt will follow. Whilst I was only an infinitesimal speck in that huge, never ending procession to Santiago, it has engraved the sense of past, present and future, and the purpose of pilgrimage, indelibly on my soul.

There was no such visible and moving a demonstration of those who have gone before, as, along with all pilgrims who enter the glorious cathedral of St James in Santiago at the end of their journey, I pressed my finger tips against the carved marble column depicting the Tree of Jesse, and physically felt them sink into the deep holes worn by those many millions of grateful, touching hands.

My journey continues, strengthened by the extraordinary and intense experience of this pilgrimage. The symbolism of the footprints is not lost on me. I am sure that my ability to recognise, follow and trust the well-worn route has increased; as has the realisation of when I have wandered off that route, and how to find the way back on to it. I also take comfort from the fact that our experiences along our journeys are broadly similar, and thus can be shared. I pray the nearer I get to my final destination I may see more people on that route; that the signs are bolder, more explicit and closer together.

Ascent of Mount Carmel

To reach satisfaction in all
    desire its possession in nothing.
To come to possess all
    desire the possession of nothing.

To arrive at being all
  desire to be nothing.
To come to the knowledge of all
  desire the knowledge of nothing.
To come to the pleasure you have not
  you must go by the way you enjoy not.
To come to the knowledge you have not
  you must go by the way in which you know not.
To come to the possession you have not
  you must go by a way in which you possess not.
To come to be what you are not
  you must go by a way in which you are not.
When you turn toward something
  you cease to cast yourself upon all.
For to go from all to the all
  you must deny yourself of all in all.
And when you come to the possession of the all
  you must possess it without wanting anything.
Because if you desire to have something in all
  your treasure in God is not purely your all.
  (John of the Cross, The Ascent of Mt Carmel)

The Power of the Way

"The Way to Santiago has created a lively spiritual and cultural atmosphere of a great gathering of the people of Europe. But what the pilgrim really seeks with humble and contrite heart is that testimony of faith which seems to emanate from the very stones of the Basilica of the Saint". *(John Paul II, pilgrim to Compostela, 9 Nov 1982)*

Antiphon

O Blessed Apostle, chosen from among the first, and who was the first of the Apostles worthy to drink from the Chalice of the Lord! O glorious Spanish Nation fortified by such a Patron and enriched by the jewel of his Holy Body, by whose intercession the Almighty has granted such great favours!

V: Pray for us O Blessed James.

R: That we may be made worthy of the promises of Jesus Christ.

Receive, O Lord, the prayers we offer you through your Apostle James, Patron of Spain, and grant that the pilgrimage to his tomb, the light of Christian unity, may prepare us to travel together along the road that leads to eternal glory.

Through Jesus Christ, Our Lord. Amen. *(From the Prayer Card given to all pilgrims at Santiago Cathedral)*

THE RETURN

"There was never a pilgrim that did not come back to his own village with one less prejudice and one more idea." *(Chateaubriand)*

Journey out of time

"Welcome back to the real world," was a friend's cheerful greeting on my return. My spontaneous and unintended reply was, "No - I've just left the real world, and I've now come back to the artificial one." On reflecting over that remark I realised how rich, but simple, my world of pilgrimage had been. Our needs were modest - as one of my fellow French pilgrims put it, our daily lives revolved round, *"manger, marcher, laver, manger, dormir, manger, marcher..."*. We carried all our worldly possessions on our backs; we hoped for a shower and a bed every night, and one good meal a day sufficed. I had no interest whatsoever in what was going on in the outside world. So, although I was delighted to get back to my family and home comforts, I was actually very reluctant to re-embrace the rest of the world at large with any enthusiasm.

I knew that I had left behind a far better world, but sadly one that could not be sustained in this exact fashion for any longer period. However, I believe that it can be replicated daily by anyone, anywhere, in small but frequent measure, through creating the atmosphere and aura of pilgrimage in seeking moments of peace and tranquillity with spiritual input.

This can be achieved at the very least by going 'to your private room... and so pray your Father' *(Mt 6:6)* every day - wherever and however that may be - even just for a short period, but employing the same single-mindedness that we unthinkingly give to setting aside the time to watch our favourite TV programme. But, unlike that TV programme there is no overt, artificially contrived plot to tempt your attention; it is not entertainment, it is a commitment. As with a pilgrim, you have actively got to take time out to make that journey out of time - even if it is only a journey of your mind for a few minutes. And once there you can place yourself in the presence of the Lord. If you want, you can accompany him on his journeying through the New Testament, or you can just amble along with other readings or prayers, or just rest in his presence.

Occasionally the benefit of going 'away to some lonely place all by yourselves and rest for a while' *(Mk 6:31)* should be sought, a quiet walk in the park or the country, ten minutes in your garden, or a Quiet Garden day, or even a retreat period. Through this process of daily prayer and reflection you can now start making your own pilgrimage - whether it be physical, or in the mind, or both - so that you can take your journey out of time, and start discovering what is truly real.

"The choice is between the Mystery and the absurd. To embrace the Mystery is to discover the real. It is to walk towards the light, to glimpse the morning star, to catch sight from time to time of what is truly real". *(Basil Hume)*

Tying it all Together

One of the strange contradictions of modern life is between that of its illusory promise of giving us all we possibly need (at a cost, of course!), and that of the widespread desire of those many people that are seeking -sometimes with real longing - that something beyond the mortal condition which can give us comfort and reassurance (and costs nothing). Amongst other manifestations of this are the ever rising numbers along the Way of St James. Pilgrimage is a practical and demonstrable way of seeking. It is a sure way of putting beliefs and commitment to the crucible. It digs up the answers from deep within. Whilst physically uncomfortable, it provides spiritual reassurance and comfort. You can walk and talk, in largely uninterrupted measure, with God. Give Him an inch, and He will show you the mile. Go the mile and He will remain with you on your life's journey.

For the simple and common goal of our life pilgrimage is to reach the Eternal Kingdom. Sadly, a great many seem to have lost sight of this in the clutter of life around us. If only we could all see ourselves as pilgrims on the difficult, hazardous and uncomfortable journey of life, and were prepared to help others, as I experienced on my physical pilgrimage, then the material world could be put back in perspective and given the right priority. In the meantime, my own small pebble is this summary of my pilgrim experience. I hope some of it will help you along your pilgrim way:

- Seek God's face in the world around you - through his creation and his people.

- Show His face to others, through yours.

- Look back at the retreating view; appreciate and learn from it.

- See yourself as God sees you. Reconcile yourself to Him unreservedly.

- Follow those clear, unequivocal sign posts along His Way. Walk past those illusory diversions to hollow self gratification.

- Try and make Self take a back seat - bring Others to the fore.

- If you feel daunted by the big ugly barriers of life, try gentle erosion rather than frontal assault - start with the smallest and easiest.

- Above all, take time out every day to make your own journey out of time to talk, walk or rest with the Lord.

Pilgrim's prayer

Dear Lord - as I start my journey today:
Open my eyes to your Face in others,
keep them open to your glorious Creation.
Open my ears to your Word;
keep them open so that I may hear what You say.
Open my mind to every encounter;
keep it open to what You are teaching me.
Open my heart to your Love,
keep it open to love others.
Give me the courage to see myself as You see me,
and to tell You the story of my life that I
have never been able to tell anyone before.

As I follow the footsteps and sign posts of my pilgrimage,
illuminate more clearly the path away from sin,
to union with You.
Allow me a glimmer of Paradise through order,
peace, contemplation and love.
Bestow the wisdom for me to relegate Self,
and the generosity to promote Others;
my desire is 'Thy will', and not 'my will'.
My daily burden and pain I endure for You;
my joy I willingly give to You.
Grant that I reach my destination this day;
grant safe arrival every day.
Grant full revelation of the Mystery as I reach my destination
at the end of my life pilgrimage.
In Your great kindness grant all this to my fellow pilgrims.
In Your great mercy hear my prayer.
(David Baldwin)

O Lord, this is our desire,
to walk along the path of life
that you have appointed us,
in steadfastness of faith,
in lowliness of heart,
in gentleness of love.
(Maria Hare 1798-1870)

Selected Biography

The Holy Bible, The New Jerusalem Bible (Study Edition) (1994), Dartman, Longman & Todd Ltd, London.

DAVIES, JG. *Pilgrimage Yesterday and Today*. London SCM Press Ltd, 1988.

HALL, DJ. *English Medieval Pilgrimage*. London, Routledge and Kegan Paul, 1965.

HANBURY-TENISON, Robin. *Spanish Pilgrimage*. London, Arrow Books Ltd, 1991.

HELL, V&H. *The Great pilgrimage of the Middle Ages. London*, Barrie and Rockliff, 1966.

MELCZER, William. *The Pilgrim's Guide to Santiago de Compostela*, Codex Calixtinus. New York, Italica Press, 1993.

ROBINSON, Martin (ed). *Sacred Places Pilgrim Paths*, An Anthology of Pilgrimage. London, Marshall Pickering, 1997.

SUMPTION, Jonathan. *Pilgrimage*. London, Faber and Faber, 1975.

RAJU, Alison. *The Way of St James*. Cumbria, Cicerone Press, 1999.

VATICAN, Pilgrimage in the Great Jubilee, 11th April 1988.

XUNTA DE GALICIA, *Room Texts*, Museo das Peregrinacions.

Selected websites

www.newadvent.org Catholic Encyclopaedia

www.xacobeo.es Santiago de Compostela

www.csj.org.uk Confratenity of St James

About the Confraternity

The Confraternity of St James exists to promote all aspects of the pilgrim routes to Santiago de Compostela. Further information can be obtained from: The Confraternity of St James, 1 Talbot Yard, Borough High Street, London SE1 1YP. Tel (020) 7403 4500. Web site: www.csj.org.uk

CTS
MEMBERSHIP

We hope you have enjoyed reading this booklet. If you would like to read more of our booklets or find out more about CTS - why not do one of the following?

1. Join our Readers CLUB.
We will send you a copy of every new booklet we publish, - through the post to your address. You'll get 20% off the price too.

2. Support our work and Mission.
Become a CTS Member. Every penny you give will help spread the faith throughout the world. What's more, you'll be entitled to special offers exclusive to CTS Members.

3. Ask for our Information Pack.
Become part of the CTS Parish Network by selling CTS publications in your own parish.

Call us now on 020 7640 0042 or return this form to us at CTS, 40-46 Harleyford Road, London SE11 5AY
Fax: 020 7640 0046 email: info@cts-online.org.uk

❏ I would like to join the *CTS Readers Club*

❏ Please send me details of how to join CTS as a *Member*

❏ Please send me a *CTS Information Pack*

Name:...

Address: ....

....

Post Code:...

Phone: ....

email address: ....

Registered charity no. 218951.
Registered in England as a company limited by guarantee no.57374.